Rules for the Traditional Family

From my grandfather . . . [I learned] good morals and the governance of my temper.

From the reputation and remembrance of my father, modesty and a manly character.

From my mother, piety and beneficence, and abstinence, not only from evil deeds, but even from evil thoughts; and further simplicity in my way of living.

From my brother . . . to love my kin and to love truth, and to love justice . . . and from him I received the idea of a polity in which there is the same law for all, a polity administered with regard to equal rights and equal freedom of speech.

Marcus Aurelius

Rules for the Traditional Family

Nicholas Puiia

Illustrated by Douglas Alvord

Lance Tapley, Publisher

Contents

Introduction . . . 9

Family Life and Roles

1. The Mother Is the Center of Family Strength . . . 17
2. The Mother Structures and Motivates Family Life . . . 18
3. The Father Provides Security . . . 21
4. Authority Resides in the Head of the Family . . . 23
5. Children Should Be Very Close to Their Mother . . . 25
6. Develop a Strong Sense of Family . . . 26
7. The Family Shares Victories and Defeats . . . 29
8. Define Success in Terms of One's Role in Life . . . 30
9. Honor the Family Name . . . 31
10. Brothers Should Be Highly Supportive . . . 32
11. Daughters Should Be Prepared to Be Mothers and Wives . . . 35

Raising Children

12. Raise Children To Be Adults . . . 39
13. Explain the Rules to Children . . . 41
14. Discipline Even Young Children . . . 43
15. Tell Children Stories . . . 45
16. Teach Children Responsibility . . . 47
17. Teach the Ingredients of a Good Marriage . . . 49
18. Take an Active Interest in Your Children's Friends . . . 51
19. Let Children Make Their Own Mistakes . . . 53
20. Nurture a Child's Interests . . . 55
21. Compliment a Job Well Done . . . 57
22. Children Should Care for Others . . . 58
23. Monitor Children's Activities . . . 60
24. Teach Respect for Elders . . . 61
25. Don't Confuse Studying with Learning . . . 63
26. Teach Strong Values to Deter Crime . . . 64

Family Emotions

27. Express Your Feelings Freely . . . 66
28. Use Humor to Reinforce Values . . . 69
29. Express Anger in an Acceptable Manner . . . 71
30. Value Confidentiality . . . 72
31. Use Traditional Values to Gauge Achievement . . . 73

Home Economics

32. Good Families Produce Good Citizens . . . 77
33. Separate Wants from Needs . . . 78
34. Prepare All Your Food with Love . . . 80
35. Plan for the Future . . . 83
36. Maintain a Savings Plan . . . 85
37. Watch Your Indebtedness Carefully . . . 87
38. Prepare for the Worst to Ensure the Best . . . 88
39. Teach Basic Economics at Home . . . 89

Work

40. Work Comes First . . . 93
41. Work Should Be Satisfying . . . 94
42. A Good Employee Is a Strong Individual . . . 96
43. Develop a Sense of Allegiance at Work . . . 97
44. Don't Expect to Start at the Top . . . 98
45. Skills Should Be Passed On . . . 101

Religion

46. Faith Reinforces Family Life . . . 104
47. Religion Must First Be Taught at Home . . . 105
48. All Children Should Have Godparents . . . 106
49. Make Traditional Celebrations Enjoyable and Meaningful . . . 107
50. Develop Your Own Holiday Traditions . . . 109

Start a Tradition . . . 111
Acknowledgment . . . 113

Introduction

My mother and father differed little from the thousands of others who came to the United States for a better life. They found a language barrier. They lacked money. Yet they were confident, excited, and optimistic.

When my mother arrived in this country from Italy, she had a few books, a small chalkboard, and some seeds of the fruits, vegetables, and flowers that her ancestors had grown for centuries. Most immigrants came to this land with little more than their skills, their common sense, their values, and their ability to teach these values to their children. But they, like my mother with her seeds, were well prepared for the future.

Although many immigrants didn't know English and some couldn't write their native tongue, they knew how to accomplish things because they had left countries and cities far older than those in the new land. The old countries had massive, elaborate, beautiful buildings of marble and granite long before the tea was tossed into Boston Harbor.

At first, very few whole families came over. The men came to work and often planned to return once they had made their fortunes. I remember my mother writing letters for these men. The letters would be enclosed with the money they sent home.

As families came to join the men in their quest for greater opportunity, they brought to this country a wealth of knowledge that, in the case of the Italians, had been passed from one generation to another from as far back as the Roman Empire. These families believed that the greatest compliment to their ancestors was continuing and maintaining the values that had been passed on to them. Cicero wrote: "Not to know what happened before we were born is to remain perpetually a child."

The United States already has an impressive history. But it did not spring full-grown from the head of Zeus. It is linked to centuries of human culture by the fact that immigrants from every part of the world built it. Yet our ties to the world's wisdom – to all our human and social history – are dissolving before our very eyes as the importance of the family dissolves. For the family is the primary instrument through which the wisdom of tradition is passed from one generation to another.

With the divorce rate approaching fifty percent, almost half of all the children born in this country today will spend years in a single-parent household. Fewer than half of nearly nine million single mothers receive support from the absent parent. Many children live in poverty, which can grind down the best of values. In 1985, there were ten million children in the United States who were poor. There are many, many threats to the family and the transmission of traditional values. According to one survey, ninety percent of eighteen-year-olds have tried drinking or illicit drugs – sixty percent drink regularly.

Each of these statistics is frequently linked to the crisis in the American family. As we struggle to understand these problems and discover solutions, too often we look only to what social services, professionals, and bureaucratic institutions can do. We overlook that solutions can be found in the family traditions and wisdom that have helped generations overcome hardship and prepare for the future – traditions that have values which are to some extent universal and not difficult to learn. They often come to us in the form of stories and proverbs. I remember well the stories my mother and father used as tools to educate us in our family traditions. This book is a practical means of preserving a wisdom that has helped generations live fruitful, productive lives free from fear.

There's a game children play. It helps establish the pecking order. In New England it's called "When Did Your

Ancestors Get Off the Boat?" After the question is asked, each child attempts to describe or invent a family tree having roots so deep in the soil of this country they might as well be fastened around Plymouth Rock. Ironically, if a child's immigrant ancestors came two or three centuries ago, they are accorded a status that eclipses even those children whose ancestors were native Americans.

My brothers and I never succeeded very well at this game. When we started school in the early 1930s, we spoke little English. Our parents spoke only Italian around the home. We were raised in Smith's Crossing, the Little Italy of Rumford, Maine. Although we knew all our Italian neighbors, the village and the region they had come from in Italy, if and how we were related, and the names and ages of the other Italian-American children, this knowledge was irrelevant to the game — although it illustrated that our heritage had a very extensive family tree.

The ancestors game taught several lessons. It was one of my first introductions to prejudice. It also demonstrated that some people believe that being an American is an inherited honor rather than an earned right.

But my father had a different view. He said that being an American was the result of fulfilling the role and duties of a citizen.

He pointed out that we Italian kids were not the only children of foreigners. The Irish were foreigners. The Lithuanians were foreigners. The French Canadians were foreigners. When we studied history we discovered the English Americans were once foreigners. In fact, only the American Indians were truly natives. The term *American*, we realized, needed more clarification.

My father said with gusto: "We are United Statesians. Now to be a United Statesian all you have to have is citizenship and pledge allegiance to the country."

Such talk – which occasionally led to monologues from my mother or father – was one way in which I, at a very early age, began to learn some of the traditional rules that formed our family's value system. I realized my role as a citizen was a big part of this set of values. I learned that citizenship was tied to personal *commitment*. And commitment was based more on personal actions than on the fact that I had been born in this country.

Although my father was a naturalized citizen and fought for this country in World War I, he retained a great love for Italy. His love for the United States and his love for Italy were like a man's love for his mother and for his wife. On holidays and feast days he always flew the flags of both countries from the front porch of our house.

I must admit that neither flag meant much to me as a child. Their gay and contrasting colors dancing in the wind that swept down the Androscoggin River Valley made them special decorations, but little more. It wasn't until I went to Italy as a GI in World War II that I came to understand the sense of *patria* my father felt for both countries and how he saw responsibility toward one's country largely as an extension of the commitment we have to our family and our community. Commitment goes this way: family, community, country . . . and, finally, to the whole human race.

During the war, I served with the 133rd regiment of the 34th Infantry Division (known as the Red Bull Division) of Mark Clark's Fifth Army. After being in Africa, I fought in Europe alongside boys and men from other small towns like Rumford. We ate, slept, worked, wrote letters, cleaned guns, and bled together. But more than anything we longed for the war to be over and to return to "our" country, which at times seemed to exist more in our collective memory than in reality.

I joined the 133rd as a replacement just before the crossing of the Rapido River in the battle of Cassino. After arduous fighting we finally took Florence on August 22, 1944. On September 11th, a Sunday, we went to Castelfiorentino near Florence. The village was jubilant, and so were we. We were being presented with the infantryman's combat medal for the action we had seen. During the ceremony I saw the Stars and Stripes for the first time in a year. It fluttered in the wind. I could see the lumps in the throats of my friends and comrades, just as I felt one in mine. As the flag flew over us there in my ancestral land, my eyes watered. In that instant, I felt my mixed feelings for my country and my heritage resolve themselves. I felt proud to defend my country and my family. It didn't matter when my parents had gotten off the boat, because I finally understood that a country isn't inherited. A country belongs to those citizens who love it, who decide to make a commitment to it and a contribution to improve it.

Part of the joy and pride I felt on that day and have felt ever since comes from the realization that it was my family that enabled me to make my contribution to society. My Italian-American mother and father gave me the keys to become an honorable and successful citizen of the United States. Their "immigrant" influence played a greater part than any other in helping me become an American. That may seem something of a contradiction, but it isn't. The responsibility one has to country and community is the result of the commitment one learned at home.

Per un grande palazzo, bisogna avere delle buone fondamenta. For a grand palace, begin with a sound foundation. This proverb of my mother's conveys the teaching that values are developed through family life and that a strong family strengthens all of society. The rules we learn at home teach us the commitment that allows us to contribute not only to our family and community, but also to the country as a whole, and to the whole world.

People change. But the amazing thing is that most of the values I learned at home are still useful today. Although many of the issues I encountered raising my own children differed from those my parents faced while raising me, I found that the values they taught and their accompanying rules could be adapted easily. And why not? If those values and teachings were able to bridge the gap between two countries and still be serviceable for my brothers and my sisters and me, they certainly could provide my children with a firm foundation for their lives.

Talking with young people — employees, friends of my children, friends of their friends — I have seen a resurgence of the belief that families and children are this country's most important resources. I think people have come again to understand that even the best experience is better if it is shared with family and loved ones. They have found that loneliness is the price of abandoning the family. At the same time, people are realizing that many of the rules of the traditional family are as useful today as they were generations ago.

Although many traditions have been discarded and many of today's young people have not been introduced to the most basic rules at home, there is evidence that people of all ages yearn for a context, a structure, a system of information that can build and strengthen not only their own families but also the society in which they live.

Some of the people struggling to develop their own sense of values and commitment feel cheated that they were not given rules at home. I say to them: Don't despair. With a little drive and a little advice, anyone can start from scratch. You can found your own family tradition! The purpose of this book is to provide you with the advice.

The teachings in this book come from the Italian tradition in which I was raised. But they have their parallels in the values brought to this land by people from all parts of the world. The rules for the traditional family go beyond ethnic traditions, because they involve human values common to all of us, from Italian to Polish, from black to Anglo.

At times these values may seem unreasonably rigid. The standards may appear out of date. Yet part of the value of tradition lies in its ability to *challenge* individuals in any context, at any time. A rule may need to be modified or reinterpreted, but traditional values give us a constant sounding board by which we can gauge our progress — or lack of it.

The rules for the traditional family can help us become better families and better individuals. But they always must be applied with love. Love is the central rule for any family.

Family Life and Roles

1. The Mother Is the Center of Family Strength

The mother is like the soul: when she is lost, she cannot be replaced. *La mamma e come l'anima: chi la perde non la riguadagna.*

Every mother is a working woman. Her work in or outside the home is love in motion. This is because the motivation behind her work, more directly than in the case of the father, is to improve the quality of life for her family. Family life is enjoyed in direct proportion to the dedication of the mother to the family.

The strength of the family depends greatly on the strength of the mother. While the father is at work or away, the mother is charged with shaping the lives of her children. In the old days among immigrants this was especially true when the father went to another country to find work which would help him provide for his family. The mother was then responsible not only for cultivating what land the family had in order to supplement the father's earnings, but also — virtually alone — for teaching the children the ways of life that would guide them into adulthood.

The powerful orientation of the mother to the family — her need for the family and the family's need for her — should always be recognized, even in these times when it is so often obscured.

2. The Mother Structures and Motivates Family Life

Long-range planning and structuring of the family's activities is also an essential part of the mother's role. Whether this function involves serving as entertainment coordinator or accountant, the mother organizes the family and enables its members to pull together by communicating the larger sense of purpose behind each activity.

This aspect of the mother's role was very clear among the families of immigrants who arrived during the Great Depression. The bulk of these immigrants came because there was a greater depression back home. They discovered there were ways of earning money honorably here. But the whole family had to work together.

The children were hired out as ditch diggers, as masons' helpers on construction sites, as farm help, or as workers in the textile mills. Everyone was a breadwinner. My mother explained that there was no such thing as "my money" or "your money." Money was pooled. The fact that one brother earned two dollars and another earned fifty cents made no difference. The money all went into the pot.

Under these conditions my mother invented a way for us to work together. It was so successful that we managed to earn enough to pay off the mortgage on the house in the midst of the Great Depression.

There was a market for berries and vegetables in our area at that time. We had some land which we cultivated. We also asked the local paper company if we could use some of their land to grow vegetables. We were able to add about two acres to our land and raised vegetables for the A & P and the First National Store.

While the vegetables were growing, we would head for the berry fields — at 5 A.M. We paid twenty-five cents to get in and picked berries all day long. That evening we would pick the vegetables that were ripe, clean them, and prepare them for market. We would also put the berries in baskets just the way the store owners wanted them. We developed a system that had us picking one day and selling the next.

My mother and father saw to it that we were transported to the berry fields and back. If for some reason it couldn't be worked out, we walked. This was a *family*. Everyone felt a sense of responsibility. This was how we managed to do well during the depression. The money my father earned was used directly to support the family. The money we earned on the side selling vegetables and berries was used to pay off the mortgage.

Saving the house during the depression was the larger purpose with which my mother motivated us. We always were made aware of *family* debts. Family cooperation made paying the debt much easier. And there was a real sense of pride that went along with contributing to the family's larger purposes. Family pride gave us a sense of great inner satisfaction.

3. The Father Provides Security

The major role of the father is to provide a shelter, a home, a place where the family feels secure. This he does through hard work, prudence, and frugality. Being a good provider doesn't necessarily entail providing luxury. It is more important to live within one's means. If that means providing only the necessities for a time, that is fine.

I remember that, as children, my siblings and I felt secure not only because the walls protected us, but especially because of the atmosphere of security provided by my father and mother.

Respect and recognition of one's father is stressed, ironically, by the mother in the Italian tradition.

My father involved his children in seemingly endless projects on nights and weekends. Working together with my father we learned the importance of both quality and quantity in work. We also gained an understanding that providing for his family was one of the ways our father expressed his love.

4. Authority Resides in the Head of the Family

You don't argue with your father or your boss. *Con padre e con padrone non si ragiona.*

It is important for the mother to recognize the father's goals and for him to recognize hers. In instances where there is a great deal of compatibility, goals will be in agreement because of the similarities in the man's and woman's backgrounds.

Still, in every family there needs to be someone to articulate those goals. In the Italian tradition, that need is filled by the *capo di famiglia* — the chief of the family. This is generally the father, but when he must be away a lot, the mother may assume his mantle.

The word *capo* has come to be associated in American ears with organized crime. But that is a terrible distortion of true Italian tradition. The true *capo* is a pillar of peace, not violence.

The responsibility of the head of the family is to communicate what is expected in his absence, what the family goals are, and how they are to be achieved. Despite the authoritarian tone conveyed by the words *head of the family,* this role is not tyrannical. The strongest heads of families are mild-mannered but very astute. Domestic tyranny — for example, if a father screams when a conversational tone would suffice — indicates a lack of ability.

In an extended family, or even a community, the *capo di famiglia* in my tradition is the one to whom people bring their problems when they need answers, not just advice. The *capo*, however, is never told directly that he fills this role. His role is defined and recognized by the actions of those who seek him out.

5. Children Should Be Very Close to Their Mother

Despite the importance of unity between a husband and wife, I believe that children, especially when young, should have the closest feeling for their mother. The father shouldn't feel disappointed by this. It is only natural. Babies are always closest to the mother. They spend much more time with her. The father is generally not so close to the children until they are older.

The great influence of the mother is seen when children are grown. My brothers and I, for example, are more apt to speak Italian with my mother's dialect. Even though my parents came from the same region of Italy, their dialects were a little different. We also know more stories about my mother's home town because of the amount of time she spent with us.

Although we look back at our father as a bulwark — the walls that are built around us, the protection needed in the event of danger, the wisdom we need from time to time — there should be a special relationship between children and mothers. This is the most important bond that holds the family together. It should not be neglected.

6. Develop a Strong Sense of Family

The family is not only the foundation of one's identity, but also the anchor of one's values. It has been demonstrated clearly that a strong family life has a positive effect on everything from worker productivity to intellectual achievement.

The breakdown of the family starts when parents don't take their responsibility of actively maintaining the family seriously. It's a matter of priorities and, of course, it starts with the children.

From the child's point of view, his development of a strong sense of family begins as he starts recognizing that the parents are concerned about his welfare on a consistent basis. The little things, such as how the child is dressed or whether he or she feels comfortable, matter just as much as the big things, such as how the child is doing in school. The child should recognize that he or she is loved and supported as part of a family. Children shouldn't worry about who will care for them.

Even though many families have two wage earners today, that does not mean the family necessarily has to be neglected. It does mean that families have a more difficult time.

This difficulty is often demonstrated in the extreme on television. In one view of the family, often involving Italian or other ethnic traditions, you see the whole family together enjoying a meal or the mother at home organizing the household. The other view shows the father picking up his briefcase to go to work, then the mother picks up her briefcase to go to work, and the child is forgotten at the table. In this melodrama, the parents stop and decide *to do something special as a family.*

But doing something together as a family shouldn't be seen as special. Being together as a unit is an everyday responsibility that we owe our children. It doesn't matter if there's one child or ten; the responsibility is the same. "Quality time" is a strange idea. *All* time spent with children should be quality time, and there should be great quantities of it.

Developing a strong sense of family in children has long-term effects. Even now I know that if I ever need help I can pick up the phone and call my brother. Even if he can't assist me, I wouldn't have to make another call, because he would contact my other brother and sisters.

This support doesn't include only external things such as financial assistance, it also includes emotional support – especially in the event of sickness or death – and it remains an important part of one's life as one grows. Even though I have children and grandchildren of my own, I still feel very much a part of my original family.

7. The Family Shares Victories and Defeats

He who has family is never alone. *Chi ha famiglia non e mai solo.*

I like to think of the family as a crack team that works together to get things done. In many traditions the reality of the family working together as a team is reinforced by the image the family has in the community. It is the duty of every family member to be mindful and protective of the family image, because what affects one member of the family affects everyone.

In these traditions, the children are taught that no matter who in the family has done something wrong, the error is recognized as a weakness of the entire family. Likewise, when somebody does something right, the whole family is recognized. The man who mentions that his brother has achieved great success speaks with a sense of family pride that results in a sense of personal pride.

Sharing in each other's glories and defeats brings the family closer together. One is never alone because the family is always there to help. A close, supportive family fosters communication among its members. I can't understand it when people say, "I haven't heard from my brother in years. I don't know where he is." In a strong family of any ethnic or cultural background everybody knows where his or her brothers and sisters are, who they're married to, how many children they have, what work they do, and so on. In recent years, however, people seem to be growing farther and farther apart from each other.

Sharing in each other's victories and defeats means that if a child strays the family doesn't abandon him. A strong family will do all it can to bring the child back into the circle of love and support.

8. Define Success in Terms of One's Role in Life

A good reputation is more valuable than money. *Meglio una buona reputazione che la ricchezza.*

There are many different definitions of success — wealth, power, fame, happiness, security — but in a traditional family success is defined most often as the honor one receives from fulfilling his or her role in life. Many of the values and proverbs I was taught as a child were designed to help me do this and, thus, to achieve my potential.

One's role in life is important not only because it creates a structure in which to work, but also because it gives one goals. All of these goals are internal. You start with the assumption that, regardless of what the world thinks, you will know in your own heart if you have achieved a goal. I was taught that, in achieving these internal goals, the external goals would take care of themselves.

Understanding how to live honorably begins when a child is given guidelines of right and wrong. As one conducts oneself by the guidelines given, one learns that there is fundamentally only one person to satisfy in terms of honor — oneself.

By violating his values, a person loses that sense of pride and honor. At that point personal success simply is not possible. Wealth, power, or fame is meaningless if you can't look yourself in the eye because of the things you've done.

The people in one's family know the individual and should know best how to measure his or her achievements. The recognition of the powers-that-be is less important than recognition from the people one loves and those whose traditions one shares.

9. Honor the Family Name

A proud family name directly benefits future generations. This point is illustrated by the importance Italian-Americans bestow on their family names. In Italy the woman does not take the name of her husband. She retains her own surname. The children take the name of the father.

When my mother and father came to the United States, my mother took his surname. That was the family tradition here. To be recognized in one's home town as having a strong family tradition was probably what she was thinking when she made this decision.

By the time my mother died her children had been recognized as responsible people and good citizens. On her deathbed she told us: "I don't go into the next world with any sadness in my heart because of what my children have become. But tell your children not to do anything to hurt the family name."

Some of the world's best-known brand names are derived from the families that originally produced the product. Just as Gucci is synonymous with high-quality leather goods, one's family name should speak of quality and integrity in the community.

The benefits of having a family name associated with quality or integrity are similar to having a letter of introduction to people you don't know and enable you to put your best foot forward immediately.

10. Brothers Should Be Highly Supportive

My mother used an expression when describing people who were close but had a disagreement. She would say, "They fight like brothers." That's because brothers have such compatibility, and feel free enough, that they can insult each other occasionally and still remain close. We were told that God chose to have us live under one roof so we would never be alone. A boy is taught from earliest childhood that a brother is one's closest confidant and that one can lean on him for support. If the brother is older, one can learn from him. If he's younger, one can enjoy being looked up to for help and respect.

The duties of a brother are basic. Brothers are to be there when they're needed and are not to interfere when they're not. It is recognized that an older brother generally has more wisdom than those younger than he. The younger siblings shouldn't fight it. They can go to him for advice, and, if he feels in need of advice, he can come to them.

In the Italian tradition, there is quite a thing made of the older children in the family. They may enjoy more privileges, but when the younger children grow up they will get the same privileges.

An important part of having a brother is knowing that you can grow up and still never feel like a stranger to your brother. I have the same intimate feeling for my brothers today that I did when we lived at home more than forty years ago.

The importance and meaning of the brotherly relationship was brought home to me in a very tragic way. The story is still very difficult for me to tell, even though the event occurred years ago.

My brothers – Tony, the youngest, and Carmelo, who was the oldest – were the first men in my part of the country to start a cable television operation. They began by leasing a mountain and putting a tower on it. Eventually my older brother decided to sell his share, but Tony stayed in the business and built a successful company which he sold to a national firm.

During vacation from school, Tony's sons Mario and Tony Jr. worked hard running the cable lines. Tony Jr. was everything a son should be, everything a nephew should be. He was a fine man. He had a very good relationship with his mother and father, with his brother, and with the whole extended family. He was loved by the whole family. He chummed around with my son Tom, who was about the same age. They went fishing together and did the other things young men do. There was a compatibility between Tommy and Tony Jr. that made them almost like brothers.

One morning Tony Jr. was stringing cable. It wasn't going to take long, and he said to his father, "See you at noon." About an hour after he went to work, he was up on a bucket truck running a line that went through a tree. As they were moving the branches, one branch went up and pulled a high-tension line down on him. It killed him instantly.

It was a great loss. It left a big hole in our family. We recognize that there are a lot of other children in our family, and we still enjoy gathering together, but there's still that person missing. For the longest time, when I'd see my son coming through the door I'd expect to see my nephew right behind him.

After the accident, I helped arrange the funeral and do some of the other things that are expected. But my brother knew that he could call on me any time of the night or day when he felt like talking. And he did. We talked back and forth often. Our brotherly relationship sustained us both. Even now he still visits me almost every day.

11. Daughters Should Be Prepared to Be Mothers and Wives

Girls in the traditional family reinforce and emulate the honor of the mother. From the time girls are five or six years old they are taught how to set the table, how to cook, how to manage the household finances, how to sew, even how to maintain the health of the other children. In the meantime they are doing things for their brothers and sisters. If our mother was busy, we always went to my sisters for help.

Daughters are prepared to be wives and mothers, just as sons are prepared to be husbands and fathers. But there is also the recognition that if something should happen to the mother the oldest daughter would be there to take her place. In my tradition, if there wasn't a daughter old enough there was usually a relative or a neighbor who would fill in. My mother always worried about what would happen to us if she died. We were told about the village my mother came from and where we would find our relatives, but our oldest sister was groomed to fill her role.

It was considered harder on a family losing a mother than losing a father. A father's presence in the home is just not so strong as the presence of the mother, because he was expected to be working outside the home. When a father died, women supplemented what the husband left by working in the home or, if they worked away from the home, they would often be able to take the work home. With the death of the mother, however, there would be the total absence of a parent during the daytime.

When you walk through the house and your mother is there, it can seem as though the house is full of sunshine. The sister can provide that same sense of warmth and happiness.

Raising Children

12. Raise Children To Be Adults

Children are a blessing and a treasure sent by God. *I figli sono tesori e benedizioni mandate da Dio.*

A pilot has the responsibility not only to put the plane in the air, but also to land it. The same is true with children. Raising children to be strong adults is both a responsibility and a blessing for parents. In the old days, children were considered a blessing because parents recognized that in their old age they would be taken care of at home, that their comfort and security would be in the home of the children. The mother and father see to the children when they are young, and the children will see to their parents when they get old. This is a fundamental responsibility of children. Reliance on government programs that diminish the responsibilities of parents and children — for example, by creating a network of nursing homes supported by tax money — helps subsidize a breakdown in the family. Let us not kid ourselves about this.

We were told that, if people were born old and grew to be children, then our parents would prepare us to be children. To prepare children to be adults requires continual shaping on the part of the parents and, in the father's daily absence, the mother must oversee the process.

Shaping the lives of children is the most important job in society. It must be approached with diligence. Phil Esposito, the famous hockey player, gave an example of this dedication when he was asked where he learned to play his sport. "At home, in the basement," he responded. "My mother was the goalie. She was a typical Italian mother, nothing got past her!"

Mothers should be suspicious. Not in a derogatory way, but in a way that recognizes children's weaknesses at certain ages and what they are exposed to. Children are not the same as adults, but there are times when it helps for adults to think like children.

My mother used to go through our pockets when she did the laundry. She would dig down in the corners like a detective gathering evidence. We would turn our pockets upside down and empty out the tobacco flecks, but we weren't old enough to realize that down in the lint there would be little fragments of our sins.

Mothers have a thousand techniques of detection including monitoring how children are spending what little money they have, noting how their eyes look, how their bearing is, and with whom they are traveling. Who the children associate with is very important. We were always told, "Tell me who you're walking with, and I'll tell you where you're going. If you go with someone who limps, you'll end up limping."

He who loves you makes you suffer. He who hates you makes you laugh. *Chi ti vuole bene ti fa piangere. Chi ti vuole male ti fa ridere.* This proverb in my tradition was used to explain a parent's sense of discipline. For example, if a child went home and told his mother that there was a party going on in a certain part of town and that certain people were going to be there, his mother would know if the place and the people were appropriate. Telling a child "you can't go" under these circumstances might make him cry. However, the people at the party who would make the child laugh are not concerned about his welfare. It should not be left to the child to choose his or her companions.

A mother's love is the most important tool used for shaping the child's life. We were told, "If you love your mother the way you should, you won't do this," or, "If you want to make your mother happy, this is what you would do." This isn't used just to impose a sense of guilt. It is a way of teaching the love a mother has for her child. Developing this fully reciprocal love is central to family values.

13. Explain the Rules to Children

I will always remember the response of my mother and of all the Italian women in our neighborhood when you asked them about an adult rule. The minute a question was asked, she picked up a corner of the big apron she was wearing, wiped her hands, sat down, and said something like, "The reason we want you in at nine o'clock is because we love you so much that any minute over nine o'clock seems like an hour. It's not because we want to deny you the pleasure of being with your friends, but because you should love us enough not to give us that grief, to find us in tears, to find us in prayer for fear something might have happened to you."

These immigrants were in a strange country, and many things scared them. They made rules for the good of their children rather than to satisfy some adult whim. I can remember my father saying, "I would give everything I've got in my pocket to see one smile on your face. I don't want you in at this hour to stop you smiling. It's that I know you don't want me to have that sad look on my face while I'm waiting for you. You could put that smile on my face by being on time. You could put my mind at ease." Constantly, children were made to think of the *family*.

14. Discipline Even Young Children

If a child is taught early to recognize the numerous levels of his parents' love, concern, and anger, the parents will have more success and flexibility in disciplining and guiding him or her through the different stages of life.

The importance of this point is illustrated by the story of the young man who had spent two years in jail. After he was released from jail he and his father were standing in the yard. His father was trying to reprimand him, to counsel him. The son pointed to a small sapling and said to his father, "Twist this." The father did so easily. The son then pointed to a full-grown tree and asked him to do the same. "I can't do that," said the father. "It's a full-grown tree." The son responded by saying, "You should have twisted me in the right direction when I was a sapling. Now I'm a full-grown tree."

It is important to discipline even very young children. You don't spank a two-year-old child, but you learn to reach that two-year-old with the discipline for a two-year-old. You don't wait until he's six or seven and kicks you in the shin in the supermarket to say, "Where did we go wrong?" What went wrong may have started when you let him rebel at two.

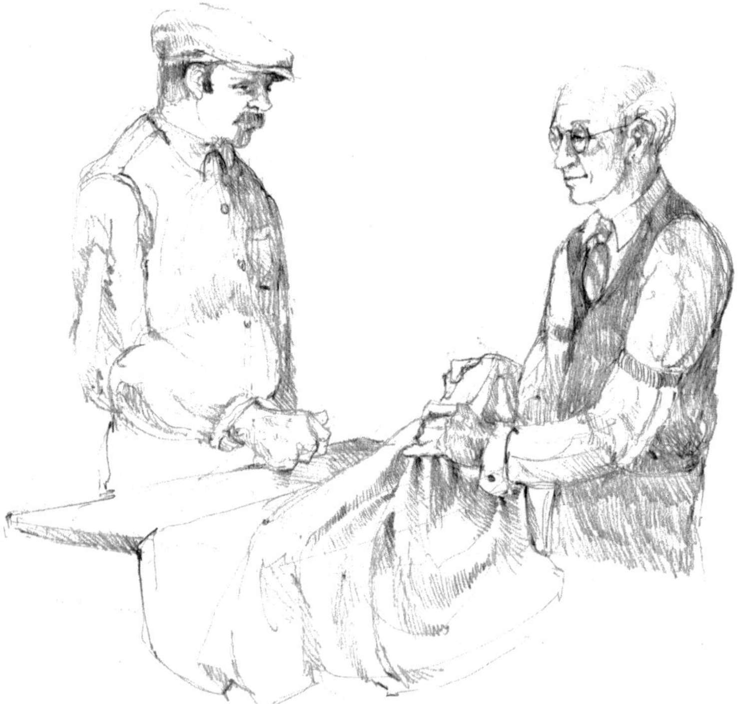

15. Tell Children Stories

Every evening after the dishes were washed we sat around and my mother would tell us either several short stories or one long story. They were fairy tales, stories about Ali Baba, and stories about life in the Middle East and North Africa (because these regions had a lot to do with Italian history). We were told stories of events in our village, our country, and in the world.

Every story had a moral. When someone had done wrong, we understood that we were not to make the same mistake. If a character in the story had done something right, we learned that this would be a good example to follow.

All of her stories were from memory. She had a terrific memory that seemed inexhaustible. Even the neighbor's children loved her stories. Once or twice a week they would come over to listen to them.

Some of my favorite stories were about St. Peter. At times he was portrayed as being a little greedy, selfish, or doubtful. Once God asked the multitude to pick up stones and carry them to the top of the mountain because He had a need for them. So St. Peter grabbed a very small stone, and everyone else grabbed the largest stone he or she could find. When they got to the top God turned all the stones to bread. The moral was that you always must do the best you can because you can't always tell how important a given chore really is.

My mother also would use humor to make her point. When God asked the multitude to carry stones up the mountain the next time, St. Peter picked a rock that was larger than anyone's. Of course, the need this time was different. God had in mind that they were to build a shelter because they were going to live on the mountain. So when they got to the top, St. Peter's rock was used only as a rock.

Not all the stories were about moral principles. Some dealt with very practical issues, such as the story about the procrastinator. There was a man who had a piece of land outside the village. In the spring he walked out to the edge of the land and said to himself, "I'm going to divide the land into six parts. I'll work on one-sixth of the land each day of the week and I'll rest Sunday." Then he reconsidered: "No, I'll divide it into fifths so I can rest Sunday and Monday."

The following day he went out to the land and instead of working he decided to divide it into quarters. He continued to do this until, as the end of the week drew near, he had all the land to cultivate. This is how the necessity of keeping to a daily work schedule was taught.

Another story that had to do with practical matters is about the man from the mountains who went into the yard goods store. He said to the owner, "I want the poor man's material," and pointed to the best cloth in the store. The owner took down the bolt of cloth and wondered why the man had called it poor man's cloth. After the owner had measured out the number of meters the man wanted, wrapped it up, and was paid, he asked the man, "Why did you call this poor man's material?"

The man from the mountains then explained: "I live quite a ways out. The trip is expensive. I lose a day of work coming to town. In fact, I have to stay over, which also costs money. The tailor is going to charge me just as much for making clothes with good material as with cheap material. Only a rich man can afford to use poor material and have it done over and over again. I'm a poor man. Clothes made of this cloth will last me two years. If I buy cheap material they will last me six months, and I'll have to repeat this expensive process four times."

16. Teach Children Responsibility

Responsibility was taken very, very seriously by my parents because they had lived in a troubled land. Many armies had trodden over Italy. People there felt a duty to take care of themselves.

In my parents' case, there was an added incentive. In Calabria, their native region of Italy, they could stand in the middle of the village and look at two seas. Each sea was on a different side of the country. Easy access to the sea had caused the area to be frequented by pirates.

(This fact led to a *garzone*, a hired hand, a shepherd boy, becoming the wealthiest man in my mother's village. He had been caught in a tremendous thunderstorm and sheltered himself under an olive tree. The rain created such a washout it uncovered Spanish gold coins. The *garzone* found crocks of these coins that were apparently part of a pirate's booty. The *garzone* lived and died as a baron after his discovery. Today the shepherd boy's family owns a tremendous amount of farmland, where they raise cattle and horses, as well as other holdings in several provinces.)

The pirates, we were told, had their hideouts in the mountains. At night they would go through the village to pick up food and provisions. The villagers were supposed to be in by a certain hour because the pirates had to be given the freedom to "shop"! One of the major responsibilities of family members was to see that the animals were safely inside and that the basement door was locked so the pirates wouldn't be tempted. Thinking of pirates made this a vivid example for children of the need for responsibility!

My mother also taught us that responsibility meant commitment and dedication. We were taught very early that when you take on a project, you take on the responsibility of seeing it from start to finish. If you were to fill the wood box, you filled the wood box, not halfway up, but all the way up. If you had animals, you took care of them.

A child's responsibilities need to be monitored. Children need to learn the commitment required to accomplish a task successfully, and, even more important, they need to experience the satisfaction that comes from successfully completing a project.

17. Teach the Ingredients of a Good Marriage

Too much time is spent on the wedding and not enough on the marriage. Preparations for a marriage should begin when a child is born. Today, those preparations rarely get the same attention as the work immediately prior to the wedding. Choosing the color of the tuxedos, the length of the wedding gown, the type of flowers, the menu, and the guest list for even a moderate-sized wedding entails much time and energy. Such plans should amount to only a small fraction of the time and energy we spend preparing a child to be a good husband or wife.

I was taught that marriage is the foundation of a life. Everything important in life will be affected by the marriage, so it is important to learn the ingredients of a good one. Obviously, much of what the child learns will be by example. But I also was taught that there are some basic steps to increase the possibility of marital success.

As much as we would like to believe that opposites attract, compatibility – on a number of levels – is the primary ingredient of a good marriage. In short, the more you have in common, the less you have to argue about. For example, Italians from the same province, who were used to the same diet, who had the same level of education and wealth, and so on, had better chances of maintaining a good marriage than those whose backgrounds differed extensively.

At the most basic level, compatibility can be examined by comparing likes and dislikes. If one likes to spend money and the other is frugal, there may be problems. Likewise, if a fisherman marries a woman who can't stand the smell of fish, then there is already a problem! A thorough understanding of the two people is necessary to determine if the couple's union is one that will be successful.

If the basic likes and dislikes seem to click, we were told, the next step is the courtship. It's called a courtship because it's a trial of deeper levels of compatibility. A courtship should familiarize each individual with the social, political, and religious background of the other. It should also be a forum to examine personal goals and such questions as, "How many children are we going to have?" and "Are we going to be strict parents?"

18. Take an Active Interest in Your Children's Friends

Many parents are not very careful when it comes to the friends their children choose. I've often heard people explain the pedigree of their animals at length, but these same people seem to know next to nothing about the person their son or daughter is dating.

Parents who take a very active interest in the friends of their children do so out of a desire to see the best for their children. That same drive inspired the arranged marriages of the past. In this respect you could say there are still arranged marriages. And there's nothing wrong with the concept.

Guiding or encouraging one's children to associate with a particular sort of person isn't unusual. We simply prefer not to call this arranging a marriage any longer because it seems to run against our individualistic, democratic notions. But for the children and grandchildren of some immigrants, the concept of arranged marriages still does not seem alien.

Less than thirty years ago members of my family were brought together through arranged marriages. In 1958 my siblings and I planned to send our parents back to Italy for a visit. We decided that my youngest brother, who was already married, should accompany my mother, my father, and my unmarried sister to Italy. It was accepted as the thing to do so he could chaperon my sister as well as demonstrate the interest we had in our parent's welfare.

When they went to my mother's village, a family approached my parents and spoke to them about their son. My parents met him. They approved of him and my sister did also. During the three months that my parents were touring Italy everything was put in order so that my sister could marry this man.

In the meantime, my brother became friendly with the younger brother of the man who was to become our brother-in-law. When my family left Italy, my brother said he would send for the younger brother of the man who married our sister. My brother kept his promise.

After receiving residency status in the U.S. the younger brother worked diligently to support himself. He turned to general carpentry when he couldn't find work as a cabinet-maker, which had been his trade. Within two years he was self-supporting and ready to establish a home.

Now the difficult task of finding a wife faced him. After much discussion, our family decided to look beyond our small locality and go to Boston with him to continue the search. There the ethnic traditions were still firmly entrenched. We had cousins living in Boston's North End, a densely populated area consisting mainly of Italian families.

Soon an evening was arranged with a family whose background was similar to that of the young man who was searching for a wife. We visited them, but, at first, not accompanied by the young man. He wasn't allowed. The compatibility between the young man and the family's daughter was obvious to us. So we arranged a dinner so the boy and girl could see each other. It went well, very well.

To make a beautiful long story a bit shorter, let me say I was his best man. From a good beginning comes a good ending. He started a small cabinetmaking shop on Battery Street in the North End, and she continued to do seamstress work. Today the man is a successful businessman, and the couple has just seen their second daughter graduate from college. We know that the basic values taught by their parents are being passed on to the children. A strong, loving family exists as the result of this "arranged" union.

19. Let Children Make Their Own Mistakes

Parents are charged with providing counsel that will help guide a child's life. This information will become the basis for self-governing behavior. For that to happen it is important to advise children without making all the decisions for them. In the Italian tradition, this activity is part of the role known as *consigliere* or counselor. When one calls upon the *consigliere*, there is usually a specific problem or question one wants addressed. One needs advice, but not necessarily to have the *consigliere* make the decision.

It is important for parents to be able to give advice and counsel without getting involved in all their child's affairs. Let your children make their own mistakes. In being a counselor and in all other matters, confidentiality is always stressed. I was taught that one of the greatest compliments one can receive is that one is worthy of another's confidence.

The *consigliere* advises on subjects such as how to be a good citizen, a good Christian, and a good employee — without ever actually making the decisions for the child. The *consigliere* simply provides information which allows individuals to make their own decisions.

20. Nurture a Child's Interests

Helping children maximize their potential is a result of encouraging them to pursue not only what interests them, but also those things at which they excel. We can't assume that education for its own sake is the answer to how to have a fruitful life.

In a number of countries, including Italy, Japan, and Germany, parents, grandparents, uncles, and aunts all spend time with children to observe what interests them. The children are then nurtured and encouraged to move in the direction of their interests regardless of whether it's a craft, a science, or manual labor.

The emotional support of the family and friends should be complemented by a tradition of apprenticeship. In Italy, as in America, professors are traditionally very well respected. But professors are not only found in schoolrooms. An apprentice cabinetmaker, for example, would still call the head cabinetmaker his "master." In the apprenticeship tradition, one works for little pay. The satisfaction of working under an acknowledged master is perceived as reward enough. It would be a good idea to revive the apprenticeship tradition. It is far easier to learn things on the job than in a classroom.

21. Compliment a Job Well Done

My mother encouraged our self-sufficiency by complimenting us for doing good work. We were excited about doing a good job because she would always say something like, "Gee, you've got that pile straight," or, "You did a nice job," or, "It's not only good work, it's nice to look at."

We also learned the pleasure and self-reliant feeling that come from providing for oneself. We raised vegetables and canned them because they were going to be expensive in the middle of winter. If we went out and got mushrooms, we would put them up in a crock. Then in the winter when there were no mushrooms around to pick, we would still have mushrooms. Green tomatoes were put in brine because they, too, could be enjoyed during the winter. These measures were not just to have summer delights when snow was on the ground, they were also for economic reasons. We tried never to go to the store for anything other than salt, sugar, flour, and other staples. But we never felt deprived; we felt self-reliant.

22. Children Should Care for Others

Children are taught to care for their parents and for others in the spirit of the commandment to do unto others as you would have them do unto you. Like many other values we teach to children, the idea that we are to care for others should be communicated in word and deed when the child is young. As I was growing up, it seemed there were always times when it was important to help others, so we didn't think too much about it.

It was understood that we would help our brothers and sisters, and they would help us in return. There was never a time when we refused to help our siblings. It was our responsibility. Even at times when love doesn't stimulate care for others, responsibility does. Sometimes it's easy to do something for someone and sometimes it's hard. When it becomes hard, a sense of responsibility takes over.

To illustrate the importance of caring for one's parents, my mother used to tell us a story about a fellow in the Far East. Long ago in a far-off country, it was a custom that when a person got old and could not provide or care for himself, he would be put into a ritual basket, taken to the top of a cliff, and dumped over. Over the years, the economy of this far-off country improved, and one of the young men was sent away to be educated in the finest schools. He did not work on the family farm as previous generations had.

Yet he was the oldest, and it was his responsibility to see that the ritual with the basket was performed. So when it was recognized that his father was not well enough to take care of himself, the son was called back from the city to put his father in the basket and take him to the cliff.

Because the son had been in the city and was not working on the farm, he wasn't physically as strong as the other sons of the village who had performed the ritual in the past. Going up the cliff with the basket, he tripped and fell against the stones. His very feeble father looked up and said, "Son, be awfully careful, your son will have to use this basket to carry you when you have reached my age."

It was then that the son turned around and went back home, where he took care of his father and thereby changed the tradition of doing away with parents who were too old to care for themselves.

Our parents told us such stories because they wanted to plant in our minds that someday we, too, were going to be old. To this day I feel proud that my mother and father lived their entire lives without ever being dependent on anyone or in want of anything. All five of the children in the family helped to make sure that didn't happen.

23. Monitor Children's Activities

An important part of discipline is simply the prevention of problems by monitoring children's activities. Both my mother and my father would take time to be aware of and understand our activities. That took time and effort, but it enabled them to foresee problems and prevent them. Being too busy to monitor the activities of one's children only leads to trouble.

Paying attention to a child's activities lessens the amount of actual discipline that is necessary. A number of levels of discipline — manifested, for example, through the tone of voice — are most effective when they are used in conjunction with expressions of love.

Over time, children learn to respect and pay attention to the wishes of their parents. Children don't always like being asked where they're going and what they're doing, but these questions become tolerated because they are understood to be a reflection of their parents' love.

24. Teach Respect for Elders

Respect for one's elders is very important and can be explained to children very simply: Older people preceded us into this world so that *we* could be born and grow up to thrive. Our elders have an advantage in that they have been *their* age and *our* age, while we have been only our age.

Usually by the time a person becomes a parent he's gone through the stages of childhood and has listened to the advice of his elders and seen what happened to friends who didn't listen to good advice. Parents must give this same advice to their children — even while they are still learning from *their* elders.

Much of my parents' wisdom was based on their understanding of history. It wasn't an academic history, but the sort of history that people with a strong sense of tradition know, regardless of whether that tradition is Italian, Greek, Lithuanian, German, Polish, or African. My parents told us that people have been around for enough centuries that there aren't too many things that haven't been done before. They often referred to the ancients and, in various expressions, to the old thought that if we don't learn from the mistakes of history we're bound to repeat them.

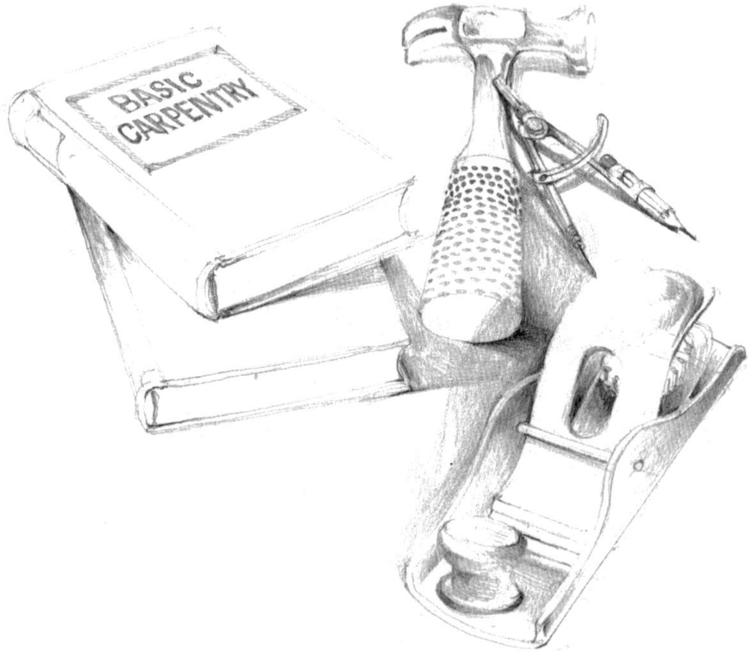
BASIC
CARPENTRY

25. Don't Confuse Studying with Learning

Some people from the National Training Laboratories, a kind of psychological "think tank," came to my company and wanted to interview some of my employees. During the process, one of the researchers said to me, "You seem to have quite a philosophy about people, about working people. How do you feel about education?"

I responded by saying I was one hundred percent for it, but that my support had to be qualified. We should not confuse studying with learning. A person can go through the motions of studying and remember what is in the book, but that doesn't mean he is learning.

The researcher asked me, "If you had one professor to pick in your lifetime, whom would you pick?" I told him that I would go to Canada and hire on at a lumber camp with a good woods operator, or I'd want to go to Greece and get onto a fishing boat, or to Italy to work with a stone cutter in the marble quarries.

A little exasperated, the man looked at me and commented, "But I said *professor.*"

"You only gave me one in my whole lifetime," I replied. "With any one of those people I mentioned, I can't fail as a human being. I'm going to learn about life. With a professor in an institution I'm going to learn about what's in books. If I haven't learned enough of the basic values to absorb that information, or if I'm too immature, a formal education will be wasted. You told me to pick just one professor. If someone teaches me about life and maturity and values, I'll be able to learn the rest, even if I have to research it myself."

26. Teach Strong Values to Deter Crime

The number-one crime is neglecting children by not giving them values and guidelines. Most other crimes are a result of that. A child doesn't go out and steal a car or develop a habit for alcohol or drugs the first time he is alone without supervision. A lack of discipline and parental guidance creates crime. Could it possibly be anything else?

We all have animal instincts, but our values help us keep them in check. Even with values, we all have thresholds of temptation. Without values we are at the whim of our instincts. Honor is a difficult goal to achieve when one doesn't know the difference between right and wrong.

If we had stronger values, and a society in which children were brought up in families to fear and deny crime and drugs, how long would the drug dealers and criminals stay in business? There is supply only because there is demand.

Family Emotions

27. Express Your Feelings Freely

Pinches and kisses leave no scars. *Pizzichi e baci non fanno buchi.*

Parents shouldn't act as if they love the child too much to punish him or her or be too timid to show their love. Using a full range of expressions is one of the true indications of love. This is not just an Italian franchise.

When a child has done something wrong, the parents should not try to rationalize it or to point the finger at someone else. If the child has done wrong, then he should be punished. This is the pinch. It isn't a beating; it is an admission that the child has done something wrong. Being punished doesn't mean that the child is going to love the parent any less. On the other hand, when the child is doing well you give him or her a kiss.

We were taught that it is important to be expressive because it conveys both sincerity and respect. This was demonstrated to me once when my father was visiting his brother — his only brother. They were very close. My mother was also close to her sister. I never saw such love. It was a good example for us. Anyway, one of my cousins came home from a ball game and walked by my uncle and my father. He said to my father, "Hello Carmelo," without even looking at him. My uncle told him to go back out and come in again. "That's your Uncle Carmelo," he said. "I want you to greet him like you mean it."

My cousin came back in and said, "Hello, Uncle Carmelo." But my uncle still wasn't satisfied and said: "You didn't say 'good morning' or 'good evening' or 'good afternoon'. There's a time of the day. Go back, try it again." This time my cousin came in and said enthusiastically, *"Buon giorno,* Uncle Carmelo." This was a way of showing respect.

Expressiveness is very important to teach children. Feeling can be conveyed by a greeting using body language. Of course, different ethnic traditions do it differently. When greeting someone, Italians give a touch of the cheek from left to right or from right to left. In other traditions, it's a kiss. Regardless, this type of body language is used to express a depth of feeling that a handshake simply doesn't project.

In Greece, Italy, and France men and women walk arm in arm down the street or through the piazzas – the men with men and the women with women. Nothing is thought of it. It simply sets a cadence for conversation and shows the friendship of the two people.

Love should be expressed and freely given as the gift it is. And, like a gift, it should not be misunderstood or viewed as charity by the receiver. Love should be accepted gratefully. Too often we don't know how simply to say "thank you." We feel uncomfortable when people demonstrate their love instead of appreciating it.

Children must be taught to be genuinely interested in others. This interest is an expression of love and concern. The best way is by example. But children can be taught to ask, "How are your mother and father? And your family?" Remember, all this must be *taught.* It is not created in a vacuum.

We must never forget how to say I love you.

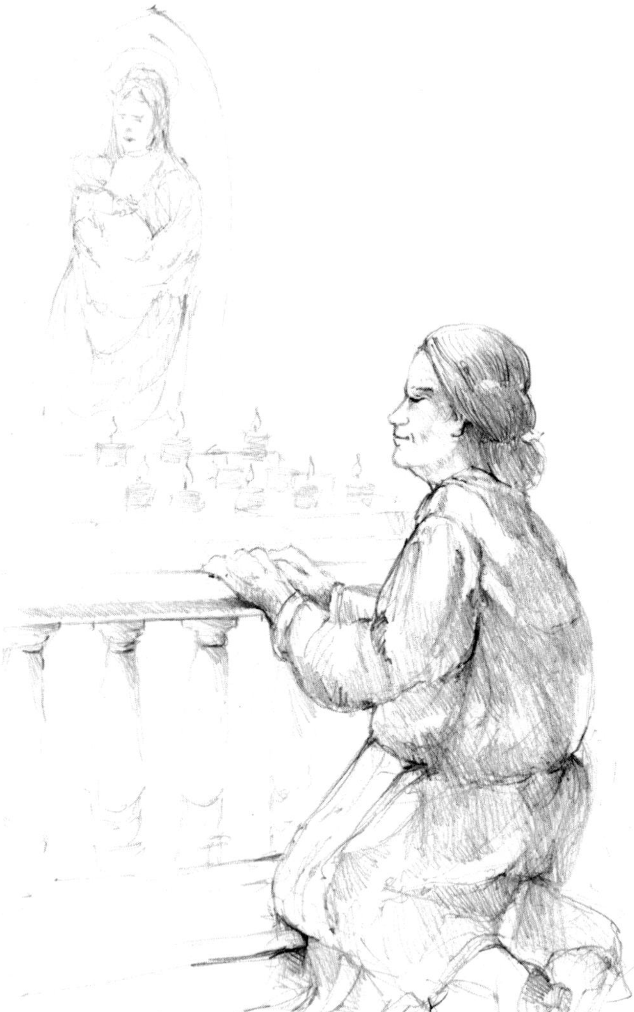

28. Use Humor to Reinforce Values

Humor often is used in traditional wisdom to reinforce values. In the Italian tradition, it is rarely demeaning to elders, mothers, saints, or to any other of its objects. In fact, there's very little humor about mothers unless it exhibits a mother's dedication or tells of the importance of mothers to children.

To understand the following story, you have to remember that many immigrants came from a part of Italy where small animals, usually goats and sheep, were the economic mainstay. Meat, these people said, was used for flavoring. If a sparrow was shot, they'd dress it out and prepare it.

The story involves a widow after the tragic death of her husband. She had three sons. She was very dedicated, and she worked hard to put these three boys through university. One became a doctor, one a lawyer, and another an industrialist. They loved their mother greatly, and they always bought her expensive gifts.

One particular year when her birthday was coming up and her boys were with her, she opened her bureau and said, "Now look, these drawers are full of dresses, suits, and jewelry that I've never worn. I'm an eighty-year-old woman! Where am I ever going to wear them? A card is enough."

But the boys loved their mother very much. They were very dedicated to her. Just before her birthday, they met a man who had a parrot that spoke the Italian dialect of her village. They went to see him and, even though he wanted three thousand dollars for his parrot, they bought it. They also bought a beautiful gold cage. Then they went to a specialty shop and bought a pillow that had the song

"Mamma" embroidered on it. As an extra-special treat, they even hired a tenor to deliver all the presents and sing the song "Mamma."

That evening they stopped by for coffee and cake. The old woman said, "I was so embarrassed that a six-foot tenor was singing to me, a little old lady. He was looking down on me singing. That pillow would have been enough. It's beautiful. I could have read the song and looked at that beautiful cage."

But she didn't say anything about the parrot. So the youngest son asked, "Ma, how about the parrot?" "Oh," she said, "he was so delicious. I had him for lunch." The son said: "Mamma mia! He could speak Italian! He could speak Calabrese!" She blessed herself, saying, "Oh, thank God! I thought I was going crazy. When I lifted the meat cleaver to cut his head off, I heard 'Per la Madonna!'"

There's another story about a woman praying in front of the Blessed Mother and a painter working inside the church. The painter decides to tease the woman and yells down, "I am Jesus Christ!" He hopes she will think she is receiving a revelation. But the woman never looks up. So the painter moves closer to the altar and yells, "I am Jesus Christ!" The woman still doesn't look up. So he goes to a point directly over the altar and hollers down: "I am Jesus Christ." The woman, without looking up, says, "I know, I heard you, but be quiet! I'm talking to your mother."

29. Express Anger in an Acceptable Manner

The admonitions to be expressive apply to anger to some degree as well, because anger emphasizes the message and demonstrates the seriousness of the situation. When a small child is about to touch something dangerous, the tone of voice in a warning is angry, but it speaks of love. Sometimes it's fabricated to be expressive, because if the same information is said in a flat voice it may not be heeded. This type of warning isn't true anger, but it is often heard as such.

True anger is the result of something that has already been done. It is not a virtue. There are a lot of things that can be done to counteract and recognize the weakness of anger. My mother always used to say, "Leave the anger of night until morning." Today we say sleep on it.

However, there are some times when it is important to respond vigorously. In these instances, if you don't express your feelings, you may never get the opportunity to do so – and it will be stopped up inside you. Still, it is important to express anger in an adult fashion and not as vengeance or retribution.

30. Value Confidentiality

The best word is that which is not spoken. *La migliore parola e quella che non si dice.*

There are several types of confidentiality. First, there's the confidentiality of the home. In my youth, a child could bring great shame to his father and family by implying that his father wasn't providing for his family properly. So you would never lament to anybody that you ate poorly at any time.

Regardless of whatever indiscretion might occur in the family, it would never, ever, be revealed outside the family. If you tell somebody else, it becomes gossip, because the minute the "friend" meets someone who is a closer friend than you are, he or she is tempted to reveal what you disclosed. Gossip is a sneaky, cheap way of imparting information. It will ultimately degrade the reputation of the one who gossips.

There is another kind of confidentiality: when someone is recognized as a man or woman of confidence. People will come and tell a man of confidence personal matters and ask for advice. In doing so, they are honoring him. By telling someone else, the man of confidence would only bring less respect to himself.

A third type is professional confidentiality. This is common as an ethical standard in a number of professions and should be common to all professions and walks of life. Privileged information is simply not to be discussed without the consent of the parties involved.

31. Use Traditional Values to Gauge Achievement

As the priest says, we're all sinners. Honor is never perfection. It's somewhere in between perfection and failure. One may have a hundred rules to live by, but only the individual truly knows how well he complies with them. As long as a person complies with values to his or her satisfaction, it is possible to maintain a sense of honor. It's hard to fool oneself, but if you're inclined to do so, try using New York Mayor Ed Koch's line: Ask your friends and family, "How am I doing?"

It is important to remember that, although it is through self-examination that you develop your sense of honor, the rules are not subject to our personal distortions. As my wife says, you don't lower the basket just because you can't make the shot. Self-discipline and -examination must be tied to some objective standard.

I follow the standard of the traditional values my parents set that have been passed down for generations. As long as I believe I would have satisfied my mother and father in my responsibilities toward God, my children, my neighbors, my community, and my country, then I feel a sense of honor.

Medals are given to people whose good deeds are seen, but there are many brave acts that go unseen. Honor is one's own reward. A rag picker can die just as happy as the chairman of a large corporation if he knows he didn't prostitute himself or subordinate his values. I would rather be a ditch digger and know that I had not subordinated my values than be the president of the United States and lose my sense of honor.

Home Economics

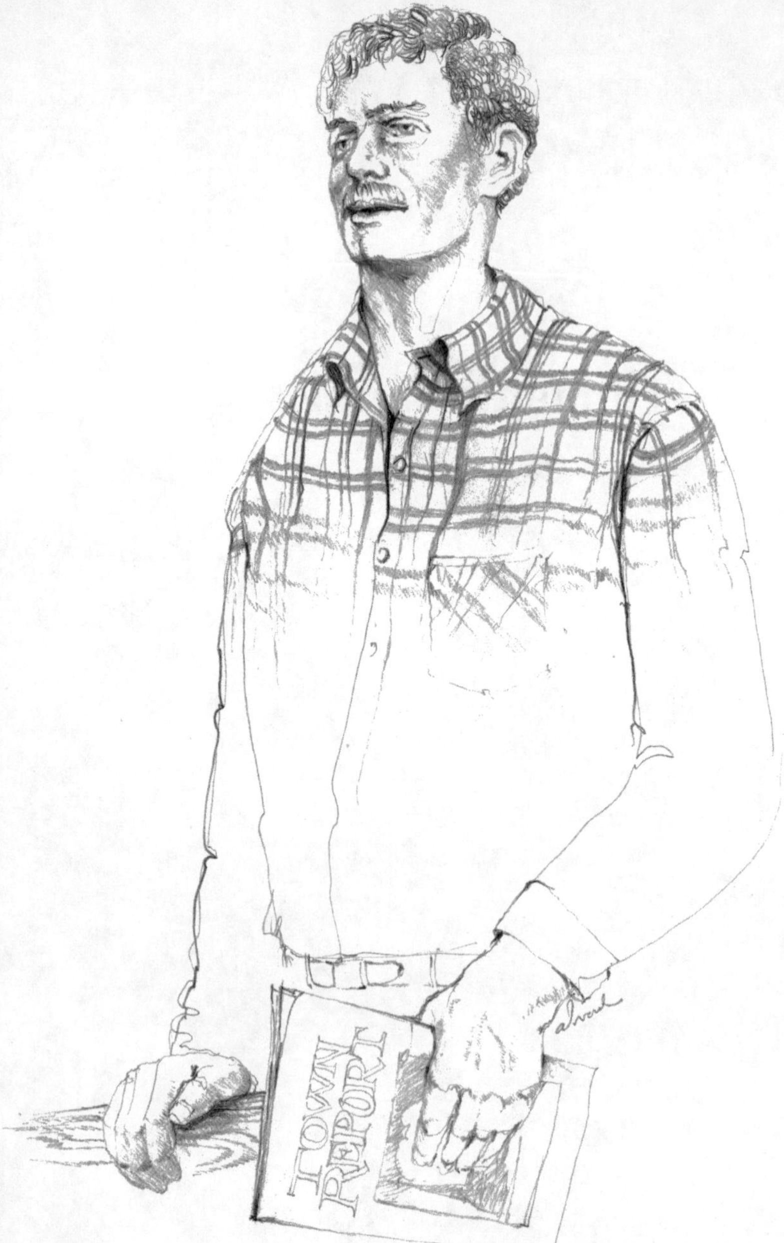
TOWN
REPORT

32. Good Families Produce Good Citizens

A strong and healthy society is like a bank account for our children. If we continue to draw on it without putting anything back, our children will wind up with nothing. Learning to practice one's civic duty is not difficult if you practice what you've been taught in the family: not to break the rules, to respect others and their property, and so on. If you follow the basics, it doesn't matter if you're a priest, a teacher, a janitor, or a businessperson, you're a good citizen.

A good family teaches that it is important to go out and work to earn money in an honest way. In such families the children have been taught to go out and produce in both quantity and quality to the best of their ability.

Without these basic understandings learned at home, it is hard to learn any civic duty.

33. Separate Wants from Needs

House enough to live in, vineyard enough to care for.
Casa quanto stare, vigna quanto cultivare.

The concept of economic self-sufficiency is simple enough. Maximize your income while minimizing your expenses, or, as the proverb implies, live within your means. Examining the difference between the standard of one's living and the cost of one's living is a good way to start becoming more self-sufficient.

Standards of living are created by individuals and can be controlled. The cost of living can't be controlled. You can decide you must have a fur coat, but you don't set its price. That is why each family must set its own standards and maintain self-sufficiency.

Today in America we're in a real crisis because of consumer debt. We are sitting on the edge of a depression because we don't have many people who know how to live within their means. At the root of this crisis is the fact that many people can't sort out wants from needs. They can't find their way back to basics.

At the most basic level, one's needs are food, shelter, clothing, and, in many cases, transportation. The difficulty we find today is that creature comforts are taken for granted, and wants are viewed as needs. Even many city dwellers today consider a car a basic necessity.

I've heard people who say they're going back to the land, but they've got to have the biggest rototiller and the best fertilizer. Our federal agricultural program showed hog farmers how to use food stamps to buy food. The farmers didn't have a garden. They were buying carrots and turkeys, chickens and eggs. In a small corner of the farm they could have raised ten chickens, but they didn't. You wouldn't have seen their parents doing that.

I was talking about the depression with a man a while back, and he said to me, "Well, we're a unique people, we went through one depression. Now we could go through another one." I said to him, "You didn't go through the depression. The people who went through the depression are gone. If we took your can opener away, you'd commit suicide."

There are families today who, if you locked them in a house with refrigerator and cupboards stocked and came back in a month, would be malnourished. But you could do the same to another family with one-tenth the provisions and they would come out fat.

The ability to separate wants from needs and to do a lot with very little during the Great Depression wasn't unique to my tradition; it was the same with the Greeks, Lithuanians, Poles, Russians, and with most of the immigrants who came here. With a piece of rope and a rock they'd make a soup and feed the family. Two meals were made out of a head of cabbage. One meal they'd boil it down and make the soup. For the next meal they'd eat the cabbage.

Previous generations went out of their way to be thrifty and self-sufficient. I remember we had an insurance policy on the house and on the children. But my mother would not have the insurance man come to the house because she could save twenty-five cents a month by walking two miles to pay at the office! Pennies were considered very important.

34. Prepare All Your Food with Love

As young children, we learned that nourishment of the body was very important. There were times when we ate a lot of dandelions, but we knew that dandelions were good food, and we enjoyed them because of my mother's preparation. She actually got them to a point where they tasted good!

The Italian tradition combines basic foods and cooking skill with hard work and a lot of love to create culinary delights.

When one thinks of preparing a meal as tedious, it's difficult to put love into the recipe. But when one sees it as an act of love and a key to being self-reliant, preparing good food is enjoyable. Rolling out the pasta or making the tomato paste by growing the tomatoes, boiling them down, and putting them through a food mill is a lot of work. It would have been a lot easier to buy it in a can, but it wouldn't have been a self-reliant expression of love.

My mother made her own pasta. Pasta quite simply means dough. Out of dough one can make fried dough, fritters, crepes, or pancakes. The basic dough started with flour and a few ingredients, such as a little salt and a little oil. Very little butter was used. My mother mostly used olive oil. She came from a country where milk was used to make cheese, not butter.

On Sundays my mother would roll out the dough and prepare different types of pasta – fettucini, gnocchi, lasagna, rigatoni, and others. Gnocchi were like shells. She made them out of pieces of dough. She'd roll them out and then curl them by hand.

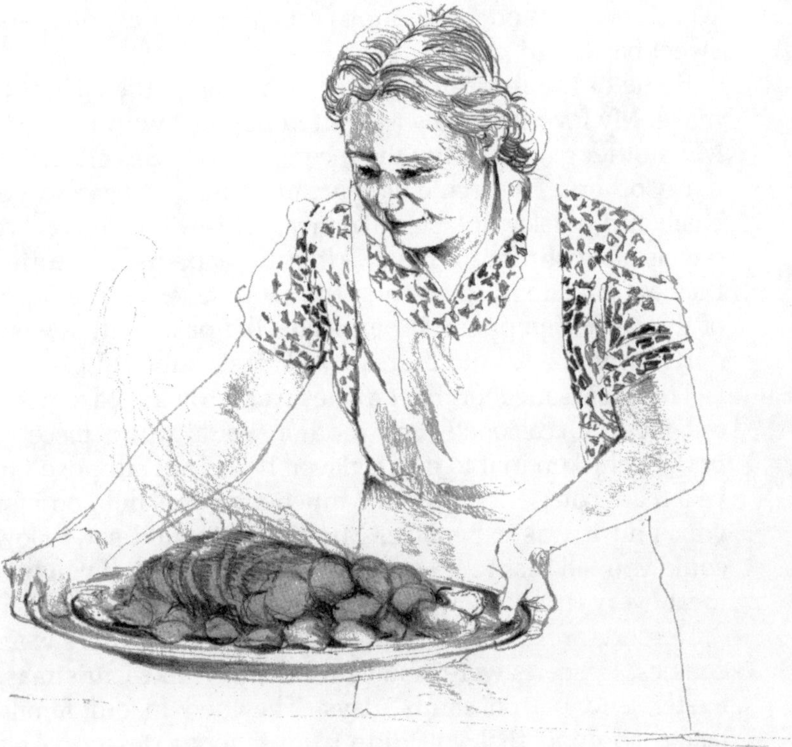

Almost all the food was prepared by hand. That way it had the loving touch and cost less than in the store. Many of the immigrant families bought a hundred-pound bag of flour and made their own pasta. It was assumed that if you had flour, salt, sugar, and oil, you could feed your family.

Regardless of whether they were urban or rural, most of my parents' friends loved gardening. They would grow things in pots if they didn't have a garden. Even in Boston you'd see them on the rooftops raising tomatoes, peppers, sweet basil, and parsley.

Some of the most interesting dishes were the easiest to make. My favorite food was stuffed peppers without meat. My mother gave my wife the recipe, and she has given it to many others. The recipe uses bread crumbs, cheese, sweet basil, and parsley. It tastes like meat. This was eaten on Friday as a substitute for meat. After the peppers are stuffed they are cooked in sauce, and the sauce takes on the flavor of the stuffed peppers. It permeates the pasta with a wonderful aroma . . . but I digress! Well, it's a subject I like.

The basic sauce for most dishes was a tomato base without meat. Occasionally my mother would put a piece of pork or chicken in it to give it flavor. It was not supposed to be a main course, because too much meat was not good for you, and it was expensive. My mother would say, "How could you tell that you were celebrating a holiday if you had meat every day?"

Desserts were mostly fruits, but occasionally there were cookies. Desserts were usually for holidays like Christmas, Easter, and patron saints' days. The food in our family tasted so good that you didn't think about dessert! And think how healthy this was.

Most of making food taste good is in the work. It isn't the piece of stone that makes a sculpture beautiful, it's the work that goes into it. The stone could just as easily be used in a stone wall. A piece of wood could be used to make a shingle or a Stradivarius. It's the work and the love and devotion that makes a wonderful final product.

35. Plan for the Future

If you want to eat bread and cheese when you're old, eat bread and onions when you're young.

Resourcefulness and thriftiness are two keys to the economic self-sufficiency that results in a good life. But they involve both planning and a sense of sacrifice, which are quite different from the instant gratification that has become so prevalent. Yet today, as we enter a new era when resources in America and the world are no longer so plentiful as they once were, the traditional keys to the good life — planning and sacrifice — continue to make sense.

The proverb above assumes that sacrifice and planning are important if we want to achieve more than just basic needs. The responsibility of providing our own needs and wants falls on our own shoulders. Wages traditionally provided housing, basic foods, and basic transportation. Anything over and above that had to be achieved through resourcefulness, planning, and by going without a few things for a while, if necessary.

Today, as American consumers, we have loaded ourselves down with debt. We have less peace of mind than those who used resourcefulness, planning, and sacrifice to get what they wanted. We are always calculating how to make payments. The desires haven't changed much. Every immigrant fifty years ago wanted a nice car, a nice home, nice clothes, and nice things for his family. He achieved those things with planning, his own ability, and resourcefulness.

To reduce the length of your mortgage, you must pay more per month. So you skimp – you eat, so to speak, bread and onions. Later, when your mortgage is paid, you can

83

afford to be more extravagant; you eat bread and cheese. The concept works whether you want to retire a few years earlier, or help your children financially, or if you simply want to feel secure.

Putting something together that they owned free and clear gave our immigrant forebears a feeling of security. That is still valid for us today. Psychologically, it feels great to be in a position to say, "I'll never be hungry. I'll never be cold. I'll never have anything taken away from me."

Sacrifice is easier when we have youth in our favor. No matter how you fall when you're young, you land on your feet. That is the time to learn to be resourceful.

36. Maintain a Savings Plan

He who goes slowly goes far. *Chi va piano va sano e va lontano.*

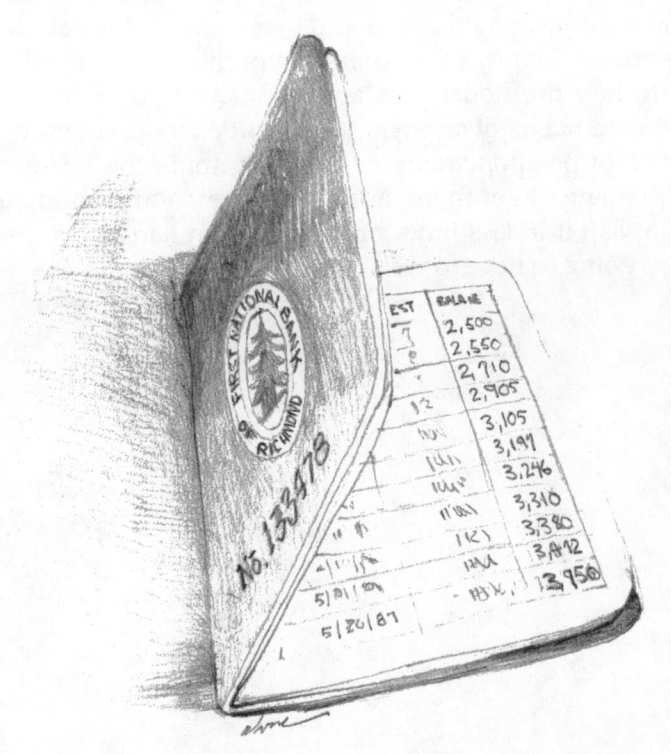

My father had a favorite story which illustrates this proverb. A stranger on his way to town stopped to ask a fellow along the way, "How long will it take me to get to town?" The man responded, "If you run your horse, it will take you five days. If you walk him you can do it in two and a half." The stranger thought, *This guy's crazy.* He went ahead and ran his horse. After a day and a half his horse dropped dead and he had to walk the rest of the way. It took him five days.

Developing and maintaining a good savings program takes time and discipline, but it pays off in the long run. It can even eliminate large mortgage payments. With a good savings program you don't need to rush into buying a home. In Boston a few years ago, six hundred dollars was a good rent, and a modest house was in the neighborhood of $125,000. Interest was twelve and one half percent. If you took that rent at six hundred dollars a month and multiplied it by twelve, you'd have $7200. But buy a new $125,000 house at twelve and one half percent interest over thirty years, and you're spending about $16,000 a year in payments. On top of that there are taxes, fire insurance, maintenance, sewer, and water. Taken together, all charges might come to about $19,000. So by renting we have a savings of about $12,000. Now pretend you bought that house, but instead just pay the rent and invest the savings at, say, ten percent. In only a few years — not thirty — you will be able to buy the house free and clear. And you will have developed habits of savings. With a little bit of economy, a little bit of postponement — by not running the horse — you're going to get there. Your goal is set. You're going to accomplish it in less time, but it will seem harder because you're going to have to walk part of the way.

37. Watch Your Indebtedness Carefully

Interest walks at night.

This proverb of my mother's about debt illustrates the point that, regardless of whether you have money in the bank or whether you owe money to the bank, interest is being calculated on Sundays, holidays, and nights. Interest is calculated on a twenty-four-hour basis. You may earn money only on a five-workday basis, but you're paying interest on a seven-day basis. Interest never stops. When you're sleeping, you're spending.

Another way to look at debt is to total up all the debt service you have, and add your taxes to it to see in real terms how much you're paying for debt. First, take your total monthly interest, say one hundred dollars, and then figure your tax bracket, say twenty-five percent. That's over one hundred twenty-five dollars a month you have to earn to pay interest. This in no way reduces your debt. So take the amount of earnings it would take to support your debt service, subtract it from your income, and you have a true picture of what your income is. There are a lot of $50,000-a-year men out there who are actually earning a lot less.

Of course, there are occasions when debt is necessary for a certain length of time, say until you get a job finished or the crops are in. But, in my tradition, it's considered an honor to have been extended credit. Someone had trust in you; he let you have his money. Debt should only be taken on when you can see that you can handle it. In other words, when you can afford it and it is not a burden.

38. Prepare for the Worst to Ensure the Best

Coming from a two-thousand-year-old culture such as Italy's — that has suffered so much change and upheaval — Italian immigrants recognized that one must prepare for things to go wrong if they are to go right. Today we call that contingency planning.

In the old days women were the insurance policy of the family. If something should happen to their husbands, they would need to have all the skills to shape the family properly. They would then have the sole responsibility of teaching the children how to become good citizens and mature adults.

There are other ways to prepare for unlikely but potentially disastrous events — for example, a simple life insurance policy and a will. But few people with children have made a will. No one likes to think of the bad things that may befall us, but the point is that if we are prepared for these things we can enjoy peace of mind.

39. Teach Basic Economics at Home

A study shows that fewer than half of our high-school juniors can identify *one* task associated with what they think will be their career. Even fewer understand basic economics. Understanding basic economics and its relation to work must be taught initially at home and then reinforced in school.

Economics creates more marital difficulties than sexual problems or infidelity. Yet most parents fail to give their children economic guidance when they are young enough to absorb it. An understanding of basic economics is important and useful regardless of whether one works in the home or in a large multinational corporation. It is one of the keys to peace of mind, because economic knowledge gives one the power to solve the economic problems which plague all of us at one time or another.

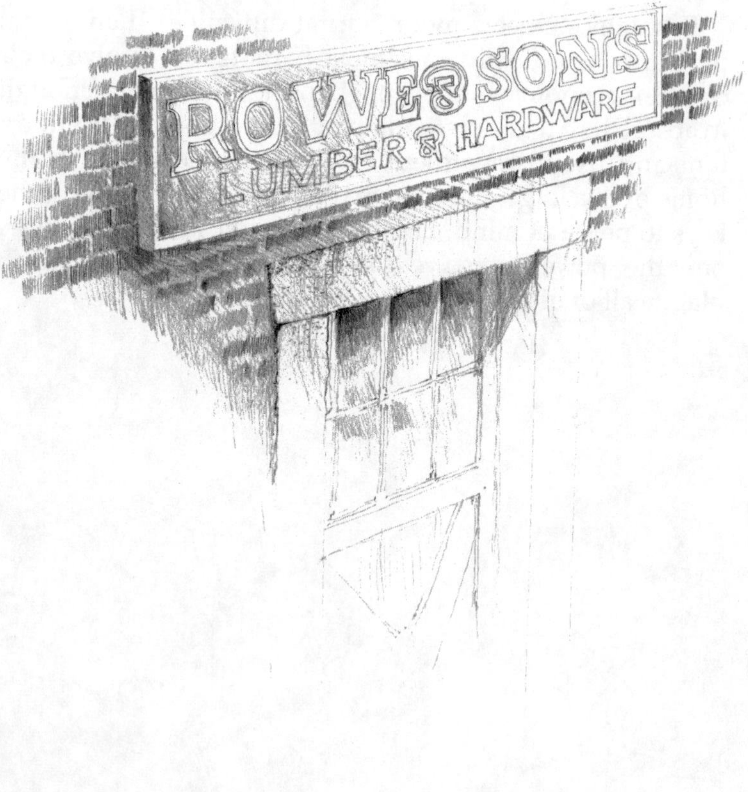
ROWE & SONS
LUMBER & HARDWARE

Work

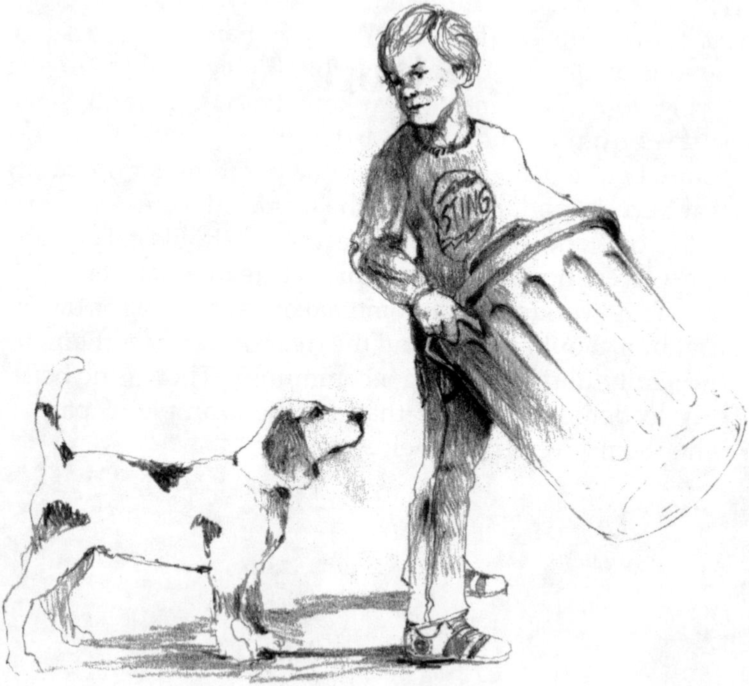
STING

40. Work Comes First

I was taught that by doing work properly one achieves several things: pride, a feeling of productivity, and the right to say one made a contribution to society. The money itself isn't the primary benefit. Working hard, of course, is famous as an immigrant tradition. Today people are also trying to "work smart." Working both hard and smart springs from the notion I was taught as a child that work comes before play. This implies that planning for the future is a very important part of the work ethic. A long-term vision of work — of apprenticeship — should take precedence over short-term jobs. This is true in whatever capacity one is working: as a homemaker, employee, or owner. Children should understand the *value* of work: for them, for the family, and for the larger community. There is no better way to demonstrate this than by the example of parents who themselves enjoy their work.

41. Work Should Be Satisfying

Work should not be seen as a burden, and children should not see parents hating their work. What an example! If one is working just for the money, that isn't enough. I'm sure that for Michelangelo or Raphael money was important, but what drove them was the pride, the recognition, the self-satisfaction and self-discipline. It doesn't matter if one is making a pair of shoes or designing space stations, satisfaction can come from work.

There are some people who are never satisfied. If you aren't one of those people, and yet can't find satisfaction in what you're doing, do something else. Work should not be distasteful. It should first of all be internally rewarding – regardless of whether you're working for yourself or somebody else.

If you can't make a move just now, remember there is no job where you can't gain a certain amount of satisfaction. When I was young I worked for a construction company helping put cement forms together. It was hard, dirty work, but it was a challenge to move the heavy forms into place, knowing that if you didn't do your job right, the rest of the project wouldn't be right. At the end of the day I would always pick up the form wedges and take care of the tools. It was a small thing, but it gave me a lot of satisfaction.

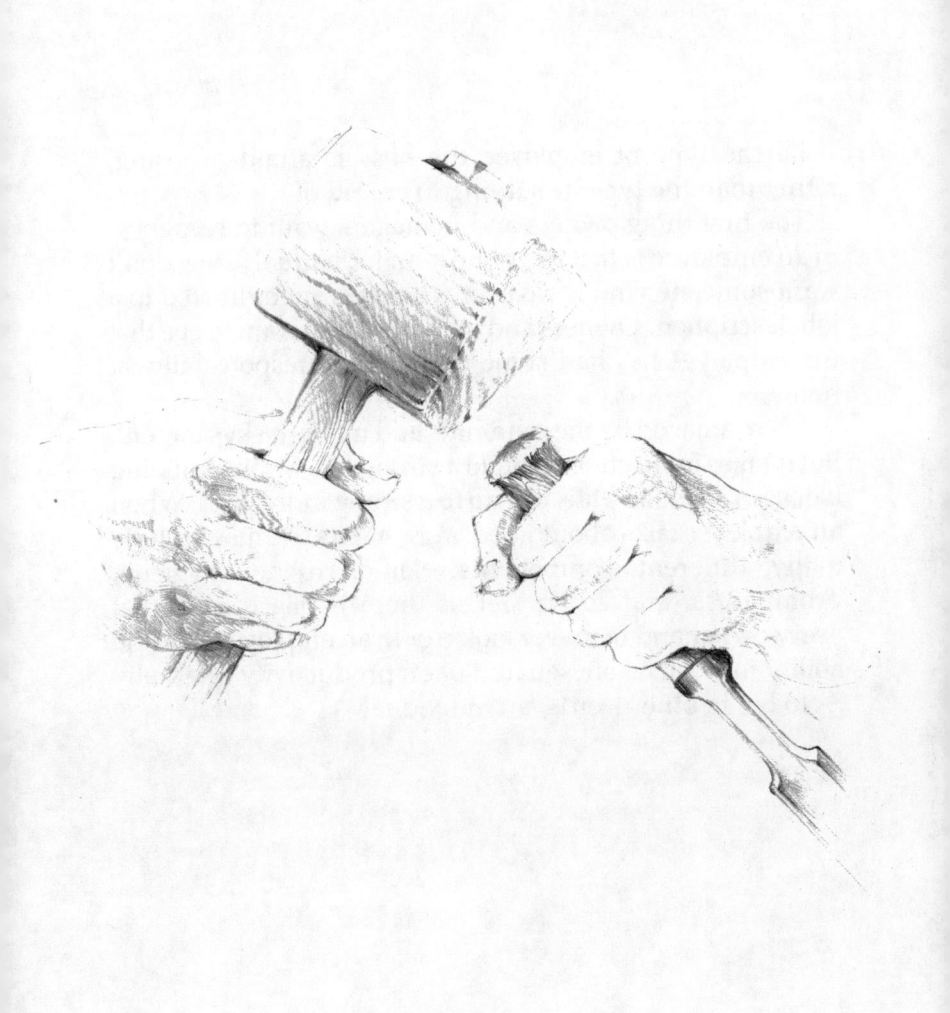

42. A Good Employee Is a Strong Individual

Be the type of employee the boss is afraid of losing, rather than the type he's trying to get rid of.

The first thing owners and managers want to recognize in an employee is that he or she is an individual. They don't want someone who is weak or who feels subordinated to a job description. Owners and managers also want to see that the employee has had some teachings of responsibility at home.

We're amazed by the pyramids and modern skyscrapers, but it takes more effort to build a strong life. Strong building blocks in a person's life add up to a strong individual. When an employer talks about good work habits, he may include many different components: self-discipline, hygiene, promptness, and so on. Yet, if there is one quality that every owner and manager looks for in an employee, it is the ability to regulate oneself and one's productivity internally — to be, in other words, an individual.

43. Develop a Sense of Allegiance at Work

Allegiance to country is an important part of being a good citizen and helps one achieve honor in society. The value of allegiance is developed at work. It is the responsibility of both employers and employees. I was given a vivid demonstration of loyalty when we had a bomb scare at my company. I came in and told everybody that they should leave, but, when it came time to go through the building, three of my men came with me. I didn't ask them to. They didn't have to, but they felt a sense of commitment to the company and, I suppose, to me. In return, I didn't turn around and tell them not to assist, because it would have been an insult. I recognized by the way they were walking and by their concern that it was their own decision to help.

At the heart of this kind of allegiance is a recognition of the value of a job and the importance employers and employees have to each other. It is much like the philosophy in Japan: Your employer almost becomes part of your family. It is recognized that, by being a good employee, you strengthen the company, which in turn strengthens the individual. This idea can be taught within the family.

Italian immigrants, like workers in Japan, and — still, to some extent, like workers here — didn't like changing employers. They wanted to be able to boast about the number of years they worked for an employer, about what the employer thought of them, and how they were recognized for their productivity. There was pride in being appreciated, and this, in turn, was reciprocated by allegiance. In some of America's best-run companies this is still the case.

44. Don't Expect to Start at the Top

To take advantage of opportunity and become an effective citizen, the young worker has to get over a sense of subordination, of feeling bad because he may be starting in a "lowly" position.

When my father came to this country it was to build a paper mill. While the mill was being built, the man who owned it saw that he had a good labor force coming here. He talked to other landowners and said he wanted to make land available for the new workers. He made land developers out of these farmers, such as the man who owned the farm that eventually became Smith's Crossing, the Little Italy of Rumford, Maine, where I grew up.

At first the immigrants built shanties on these pieces of land because they couldn't afford mortgages. Many of them were convinced that they weren't going to stay here, anyway. They were going to go back to Italy after they made their bundle. But later they decided to send for their wives, or they went back and got married and returned with wives.

When the mill was finished, the construction crews disbanded and the men worked on the production lines or pulpwood unloading crews. For most, it didn't matter whether they were digging a ditch or shoveling sulphur and lime out of a boxcar. It was a job, and they were good workers. They were loyal, and they felt they would be rewarded for their effort.

Although the structure of work in America has changed, and it is more difficult to work one's way up the ladder in a single organization, it is still important to remember that no one starts at the top. The beauty of working in America is that, in most sectors of the economy, it is still possible to advance through achievement. It may take moving to a different company or starting one's own, but with the right attitude it can be done.

An attitude of respect for one's employment — which means respect, too, for one's employer — begins with instruction in the home on the value of work. As an employer, I will be suspect for promoting respect for employers, but all I am saying is that *everyone* deserves respect. Employers should not be viewed as enemies. That is a terrible instruction to children.

45. Skills Should Be Passed On

One of the important things I was taught about work is that skills should be passed on from one generation to another without a decrease in quality. If you stay in the same trade or the family business, two generations may be working side by side until one phases out and the other phases in. The customer should never notice any loss in quality.

If a child goes into another trade, he or she should be put in the hands of a master. My father was a cobbler. I didn't want to be a cobbler, so I apprenticed with a plumber and carpenter. Regardless of whether the work is taught by a master to an apprentice or by a father to his son, the skillful qualities of the work must be passed on. The loss of the apprenticeship tradition is a great mistake. It has resulted in less-satisfying work and lower-quality goods and services. But, although society appears to have gone another way, I suggest that the individual family can single-handedly revive it! It would be a very unusual but very beneficial thing if you apprenticed your teenaged boy or girl to someone who carried on an art, a craft, a trade, or a business in which the child was interested. These days, children, who have great powers of absorption, are often denied the chance to learn something deeply, to feel useful and productive, and to feel as though they are on a course that will benefit them throughout their lives.

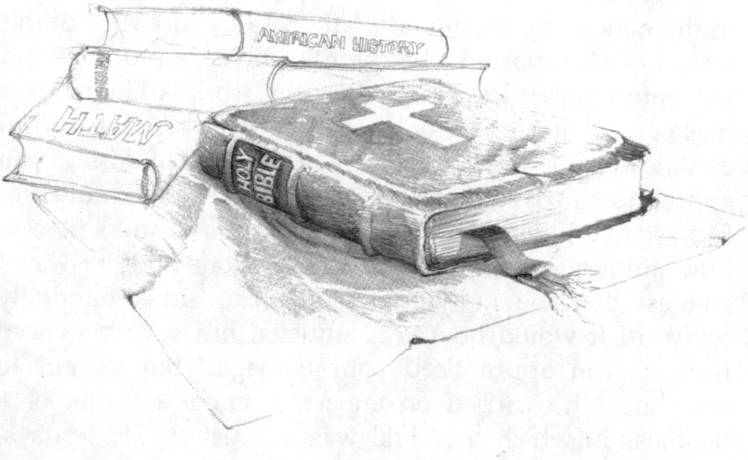
AMERICAN HISTORY
MATH
HOLY
BIBLE

Religion

46. Faith Reinforces Family Life

Whether the rooster crows or not, God brings the daylight. *Gallo o non gallo, Dio fa giorno.*

We have to believe in something. Some people call it nature. Some call it God. Regardless of one's past or one's lack of belief, in the event of a crisis people often go to church and try to communicate with God.

In my tradition we see faith in God as a central part of a successful life, especially of a successful family life. But we also see that faith without work is not enough. My mother used to say: "You say rosaries but you also haul fertilizer to your garden."

Prayers to God are only part of exercising your faith. There's a responsibility on your part. Faith may be the driving force, but put your plans in motion.

Exercising one's faith doesn't mean a fanaticism about religion. It is simply a recognition of the fact that religion is essential to life. A sense of tradition would be impossible without faith, and *vice versa*. One reinforces the other.

47. Religion Must First Be Taught at Home

Religion in my tradition was taught in the home and then reinforced in church. The importance of religion as a critical element in one's life was assumed. But in recent generations religion has become secondary for many people. Its importance has not always been taught or passed on. Our society has begun to show the effects. Religion in America was an important method of shaping and refining the morality of future generations. The weakening of this force has resulted in a weakening of our society.

The positive signs are that young people are to some extent returning to religion. If, here and now, we are to effect positive changes and improvements in society for our children and grandchildren, religion must play a role in our lives and in their lives. Our spiritual needs join with our social responsibilities.

The best way to teach religion at home is of course to live a good life. We don't seem to understand in our society that *everything* is taught to children — especially what we do rather than what we say. But, also, if we don't explicitly teach children the connection between religion and family values, they will not fully appreciate those values, and they will not fully appreciate religion.

48. All Children Should Have Godparents

The practice of naming godparents was developed in the early Christian church because members of the faith were persecuted and often killed. The uncertainty of their lives led believers to invite Christian friends or relatives to make a solemn promise to raise the child in the faith. That responsibility still holds for godparents today. They are charged with seeing that the child is brought up in the faith and in a worshiping community.

The role of godparents implies that they have reaffirmed their own faith and promised to care for the godchild's well-being. The role also implies that the godparents will help the parents fulfill their Christian responsibilities toward the child.

Specific things godparents can do include participating in the child's baptism, remembering the child in prayer and at his or her birthday or baptism anniversary, providing materials to develop the child's faith, and inviting the child to spend time with them.

Even if you are not a practicing Christian, or a Christian at all, you can still "invent" the relationship of godparents. It is, finally, an expression of love.

49. Make Traditional Celebrations Enjoyable and Meaningful

Our faith is worked into our daily lives in many ways, but when I was growing up one of the most exciting ways religion mixed with tradition was the celebration of religious holidays and feast days of the saints. My mother was very inventive in the ways she would merge her faith and seasonal events. She always did it in a manner that would involve the children. We learned to enjoy the meaning behind the tradition as well as the festivities themselves. We weren't allowed to forget that it is ultimately because of God's abundance and forgiveness that we can celebrate anything.

On May Day, the first of May, my mother would tell us that the day commemorated when the Blessed Mother gave the baby Jesus seven different gifts, one for each day of the week. We would come down in the morning and see five little bags on the counter. In each there were seven different items. They might be candies, apples, or something my mother had baked, but there were seven *different* things.

For holy days such as Easter, St. Rocco's, or St. Anthony's, there would be lots of cooking ahead of time. Different breads, sweetbreads, numerous pastas, and special meats such as veal cutlets were prepared. And there was special music that was practiced during the rest of the year. There were also movable feasts. If you had your cousins over one day, you went to their house another day.

Many people of English descent in our town saw the Italians as one people. We saw ourselves as people who had come from all over Italy, with different customs and different foods. So the night before special days such as Easter, Christmas, and New Year's we would exchange dishes of food to celebrate the bounty God had given us and to get to know each other's traditions. You would see kids walking around the neighborhood carrying dishes with white cloths over them.

The anticipation and preparation for holidays should be enjoyed as much as the celebrations themselves. I remember how we would get home from school and smell the different things my mother was cooking. The household was full of light, excitement, and those wonderful aromas. We'd want to get into the food, but she'd say, no, no. Yet she would always give us a little taste.

50. Develop Your Own Holiday Traditions

There are many holiday traditions. They carry a sense of meaning of the holiday and of history. But occasionally the meaning gets lost. It is possible to add meaning to a holiday by developing your own traditions or reviving those of the past.

A tradition my mother made her own was the shrine and vigil light. She used to take a cup, almost fill it with water, and then add about a half inch of olive oil. Then she would put tiny wax things in it with a little piece of wood to be ignited. My mother had one going all of my life. In the morning you could hear the flame sizzling because it had used up the oil and was reaching the water. The vigil light was always in front of a statue of the Blessed Mother. On the feast days my mother would have one in front of our statue of a saint. We celebrated our feast days with more vigor than our birthdays.

A special tradition we had in place of Thanksgiving was a winemaking day that was a celebration of God's bounty. Several families would buy seventy-five, a hundred, or even a hundred and fifty boxes of grapes of different types. While we made the wine, we could eat all the grapes we wanted.

To begin, we would step into a large washtub wearing boots that had been washed and placed in another tub of clean water. We would mash the grapes and then put them in barrels to start fermenting. We didn't use a press until the end of the process. At this point, we would simply squeeze the grapes and put the grapes and juice in wooden casks. Then, after so many days, the foam would bring everything but the juice to the top, and we would draw the first wine. The second wine was made by putting a block of wood and a rock on top of what was left in the cask, letting the weight squeeze out the juice. After that, we would take all that was left and put it in a press. Because we would press the stems and the pits, this last would be a wine of lesser quality. When the wine cleared, we would put it in barrels on their sides, wait until it foamed at the top, then put putty around the bunghole to seal the barrel. Then we would let it age.

Tasting the new wine usually occurred around Christmas. It was just as eventful as making the wine. It was part of the tradition that the family of one's uncle or one's godparents would come over, and they would draw a pitcher of the new wine. In a day or two you'd find yourself in one of your relatives' houses watching the same thing happen.

Today, new traditions can replace the old. They are such an important part of establishing and maintaining the family unity. They are also an important means of integrating one's faith into daily life.

Start a Tradition

Know the custom, not the costume. *Paese che vai, usanze che trovi.*

It is important to recognize the values that have brought us this far as a nation and as a civilization. We must respect those values. They can continue to provide us with a basis for personal and societal success. That's why generation after generation has held onto them, regardless of how they are phrased.

Even if one wasn't raised with a strong set of values, one's life can still be founded on them. The rules in this book reflect some of those fundamental values. By knowing the fundamentals one finds that almost everything else will take care of itself. Even if you haven't come from a strong, family-oriented tradition, you can start your own tradition with these fundamentals. Regardless of how we express them — in Italian, English, or Farsi — people know when strong, traditional values are being followed and when they have been compromised. The fact that some of our values have been sold short today doesn't mean those of our children have to be.

A person doesn't have to ponder too deeply to come up with the rules of how to be a good citizen and a good person. If you structure your life to follow these rules, you've got a foundation started for your children and grandchildren.

The Chinese have always felt that they could not correct major social problems with the present generation because the values of adults have already been formed. So they structure change to occur with the next generation. That doesn't mean that the people of this generation do not contribute to the change. They help to create it.

To start a tradition, we need to look closely at ourselves and our responsibilities to our children. Our most basic responsibility is to our children. Through them we look beyond ourselves to society as a whole.

Traditional values are not just important to my family tradition or your family tradition, they are important to the human family. Love of children, home, and country are not outdated beliefs. They are the basis for bringing the world closer together.

Acknowledgment

To my mother, Rosaria Laugelli Puiia, whose wisdom rivaled Solomon's. She instilled in me the belief that honor, above all, should be the guide to life.

To my father, Carmelo S. Puiia, whose "old world" teachings met the test of time and passed it.

To Francesco and Caterina Penna, my extended family in Rome, Italy; and in the United States, Thomas and Catherine "Kitty" Salzarulo. The dedication of these couples to each other and to their children made an indelible impression in my mind of what "family" is all about.

To Jim Kupel, the scribe and editor of this book. This is his book as well as mine.

Nicholas Puiia was born in 1925 in Rumford, Maine, the son of Italian immigrants. He graduated from Rumford High School into the Second World War and saw combat with the 34th infantry division of Mark Clark's Fifth Army in Africa and Europe.

After the war he returned to Rumford and began a highly successful business career. He and his wife, Dorothy, have eight children and almost as many grandchildren. One of his great pleasures is returning on extended visits to the country of his ancestors. This is his first book.